Gun Safety

By
Sammy Franco

Also by Sammy Franco:
Out of the Cage: A Complete Guide to Beating a Mixed Martial Artist on the Street
Heavy Bag Training: Boxing - Mixed Martial Arts - Self Defense
Warrior Wisdom: Inspiring Ideas from the World's Greatest Warriors
Judge, Jury and Executioner
Savage Street Fighting: Tactical Savagery as a Last Resort
Feral Fighting: Level 2 WidowMaker
Ground War: How to Destroy a Grappler in a Street Fight
The Combat Conditioning Workout Journal
War Blade: A Complete Guide to Tactical Knife Fighting
The WidowMaker Program: Maximum Punishment for Extreme Situations
War Craft: Street Fighting Tactics of the War Machine
War Machine: How to Transform Yourself Into a Vicious and Deadly Street Fighter
The Bigger They Are, The Harder They Fall: How to Defeat a Larger & Stronger Adversary in a Street Fight
First Strike: Mastering the Preemptive Strike for Street Combat
1001 Street Fighting Secrets: The Principles of Contemporary Fighting Arts
When Seconds Count: Everyone's Guide to Self Defense
Killer Instinct: Unarmed Combat for Street Survival
Street Lethal: Unarmed Urban Combat

Gun Safety: For Home Defense and Concealed Carry
Copyright © 2013 by Sammy Franco
ISBN 978-0-9890382-3-2
Printed in the United States of America

Published by Contemporary Fighting Arts, LLC.
P.O. Box 84028
Gaithersburg, Maryland 20883 USA
Call Toll Free: 1-(877) 232-3334
Visit us online at: www.sammyfranco.com

For author interviews or publicity information, please send inquiries in care of the publisher or visit the CFA web site at: www.sammyfranco.com

TABLE OF CONTENTS

Important!

The information and techniques presented herein can be dangerous and could result in serious injury. The author, publisher, and distributors of this book disclaim any liability from loss, injury, or damage, personal or otherwise, resulting from the information and procedures in this book. This book is for academic study only.

CHAPTER ONE

Gun Ownership

Why People Own Firearms

Millions of Americans own firearms for a variety of reasons: personal protection, home defense, recreation, hunting, collecting, and competition. Interestingly enough, the number of women owning firearms has increased dramatically to more than 12 million.

Overall, we know that firearm ownership is a controversial issue that has generated tremendous national concern. Some pro gun activists believe that law-abiding citizens have an absolute Constitutional right to bear arms with restrictions. Their opponents, on the other hand, believe that guns are the root of all evil and must be eliminated to address criminal violence in our society effectively.

People own firearms for a variety of reasons. In this photo, the practitioner participates in a shooting competition.

My opinion on firearm ownership is simple. I think firearms have a very real place in self defense and personal protection. So long as there are deadly and vicious criminals, there is a need for firearms. Yet I don't believe everyone should own a gun. It's pretty hard to disagree with the position that gun ownership should be restricted to law-abiding citizens who are willing to make the time and commitment to safe, responsible ownership.

The decision to own a firearm for personal protection warrants considerable thought and honest reflection. Here are some important questions to ask yourself:

- Do you abuse alcohol or use drugs?

- Are you hot tempered?

- Could you take the life of another human being?

- Are you subject to long periods of depression?

- Do you live alone?

7

- Are there children in your household?

- Why do you want a gun?

- Have you ever shot a gun?

- Are you a disorganized person?

- Are you accident prone?

- Are you willing to take the time to obtain the knowledge and learn the skills needed to handle firearms safely?

"It's pretty hard to disagree with the position that gun ownership should be restricted to law-abiding citizens who are willing to make the time and commitment to safe, responsible ownership."

If you are going to own a firearm, you must learn to use it properly. This means lots of time at the gun range.

I hope you get my point. You'd better sit down and have a serious face-to-face talk with yourself before you even visit the gun shop. And remember these scary truths about firearms: many gun owners are killed accidentally by their own weapons, and handguns and shotguns contribute significantly to the death of friends and family members.

> *"Many gun owners are killed accidentally by their own weapons, and handguns and shotguns contribute significantly to the death of friends and family members."*

Gun ownership carries tremendous social responsibilities. You must be knowledgeable of the circumstances that could justify the use of a firearm in self defense. However, the laws concerning firearm usage are not something you're going to learn overnight. Using a firearm for self defense is legally complex.

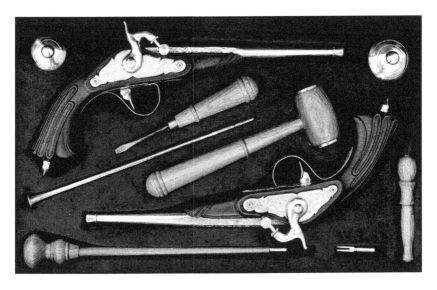

Consider, for example, the scary fact that it is not always justified to use a gun against an intruder in your home. This fact is hard to believe or accept, but it's true. A gun places you in the position of judge, jury, and executioner—all in a matter of seconds.

You are no more qualified to use a gun because you've purchased one than you are to conduct a Beethoven symphony because you own the sheet music. If you are going to own a firearm, learn to use it properly. Get qualified training in safe handling, basic operation and maintenance, and marksmanship. Ideally, children and other family members should be trained as well. Remember the fallacy of dependency. A gun may not always be there when you need it most, so don't be solely reliant upon one for your or your family's safety. You have to figure out a way to make it readily accessible to you but safely away from the hands of unauthorized people.

The Gun Safety handbook was specifically written to address the critical issue of safe gun handling. The truth of the matter is gun accidents can be completely avoided if you act responsibly and follow the rules and guidelines presented in this book.

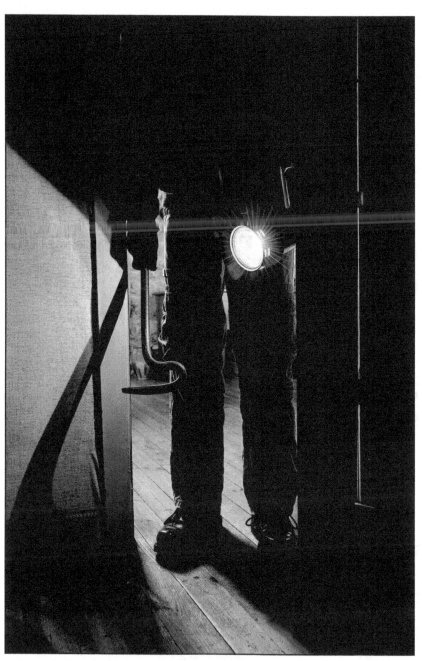

Are you and your family prepared for this possible scenario?

The Pros and Cons of Gun Ownership

In the hands of a trained citizen, a firearm is the ultimate weapon in most circumstances. If you are technically skilled in its use and psychologically prepared to use lethal force, the gun has a real place in your world of self defense. Imagine waking up in the middle of the night to the horrifying sound of a criminal breaking into your home. Having a gun in your bedroom might save your life.

> *"Imagine waking up in the middle of the night to the horrifying sound of a criminal breaking into your home."*

Firearms do have a significant deterrent effect on crime. According to the U.S. Justice Department, an armed citizen is more likely to escape rape, robbery, and assault than an unarmed citizen. The Justice Department also found that a citizen who is armed with a firearm is twice as likely to avoid injury during a robbery than his or her unarmed counterpart.

For example, in Anniston, Alabama, Ben Taylor and his wife had been terrorized for years by a man who regularly stole their Social Security money. When the man's attacks became increasingly violent, Mr. Taylor armed himself with his friend's .38-caliber handgun. When the assailant showed up at the house again and kicked through the door, Mr. Taylor fired twice, killing the criminal intruder.

In some circumstances the mere presence of a firearm may allow you to gain control and command over a criminal without firing the weapon.

"If you are technically skilled in its use and psychologically prepared to use lethal force, the gun has a real place in your world of self defense."

Criminologist James Wright of the University of Massachusetts conducted a study of 1,800 convicted felons. His study revealed the following:

- 57 percent of the felons interviewed said they were frightened by an armed citizen.

- 53 percent said they would not commit a crime if they believed a citizen was armed.

- 60 percent indicated they were more concerned about being shot by an armed citizen than by the police.

The bottom line is, bad guys are afraid of guns in the hands of a citizen.

"The Justice Department also found that a citizen who is armed with a firearm is twice as likely to avoid injury during a robbery than his or her unarmed counterpart."

A gun is the great equalizer because it converts the neutral zone to a range of deadly engagement beyond the criminal's reach.

Against overpowering deadly force, a gun is the great equalizer because it converts the neutral zone to a range of deadly engagement beyond the criminal's reach. A gun gives you the psychological and physical force to protect yourself and your family. A firearm also provides protection to people who are physically handicapped or too weak to protect themselves against a violent criminal.

For example, a gun in the hands of a trained paraplegic will instantly give him the power and strength of a small army. A firearm can also make a small female far more powerful than a stronger male aggressor. For example, a semiautomatic handgun provided protection for a woman in New Orleans. After calling the police to report a prowler outside her home, the woman got her gun, and when the large intruder entered through her front door, she shot him in the neck, putting him into flight. Minutes later, the wounded suspect was apprehended by the police.

"The bottom line is, bad guys are afraid of guns in the hands of a citizen."

In some circumstances the mere presence of a firearm may allow you to gain control and command over a criminal without firing the weapon.

Consider the story of a Yonkers, New York, woman who was making a call at a public phone when a strong armed robber demanded her purse. Instead she reached into her purse and came out with her licensed .38 revolver. The criminal fled empty-handed. A gun can tilt the balance of power significantly in your favor. But you must be trained and prepared to use it.

A firearm is the ultimate self defense equalizer because it offers any person, regardless of age, sex, and strength the ability to deliver deadly force.

While the police do the best they can to protect us from violent criminals, the truth is we are each individually responsible for protecting ourselves and our families.

Buying a Firearm

Before you buy a gun, it is your responsibility to understand and obey the various laws governing its use, possession, and transportation. Such laws vary from state to state, so learn the ones that apply to you and your community. Your local police or sheriff's department can tell you.

Purchasing a firearm is not going to be easy. With so many different guns on the market, it is often difficult to make a choice. However, here are some important questions that will help you with your selection.

- What purpose will the gun serve?

- Will it be used for hunting, target practice, or self defense?

- Are you interested in a shotgun, semiautomatic, or revolver?

- How much money are you willing to spend?

Also consider these helpful tips before buying a gun for personal protection:

1. Get advice from firearm experts, police officers, and reputable dealers.

2. Familiarize yourself with the various models on the market.

3. Read various gun magazines and find out which guns have the greatest reliability.

4. Read the warranty or guarantee that comes with the firearm.

5. Look for high-quality brand-name firearms.

6. Know the gun's recoil before you buy it.

7. Buy the firearm from a reputable dealer.

8. Be certain the firearm fits comfortably in your hand.

9. Look for a gun that is easy to clean and operate.

10. Be certain the weapon has sufficient "stopping power".

"Before you purchase a handgun for home defense and self defense, it is your responsibility to understand and obey the various laws governing its use, possession and transportation."

One important consideration when buying a gun for self defense is the weapon's recoil.

Avoid impulsive purchases because firearms can be very expensive and cannot be returned to the gun shop. If there is a particular gun that interests you, spend some time and do some research on the weapon. Be patient, it takes time to research a gun purchase.

You can buy firearms from some of the following locations:

- Sporting Good Store
- Independently Owned Gun Shops
- Big Box Stores
- Gun Shows
- Online

CHAPTER TWO

Gun Safety

The 4 Standard Safety Rules

Let me be clear from the start, guns do not kill people, it's people that kill people. I know it sounds cliche, but it's the truth! Guns simply don't discharge by themselves! They are inanimate objects. It's the human element that makes them dangerous!

Now, if you are considering owning a gun you must never forget that firearm ownership is a full-time responsibility. A gun is inherently dangerous to you and everyone around you. If you are an untrained or irresponsible gun owner, you may be more dangerous to yourself and your family than a potential criminal.

The truth of the matter is guns kill innocent people if they are not properly stored and handled. Most firearm accidents are attributed to ignorance and carelessness.

- Ignorance means that you are unaware of the standard firearm safety rules.

- Carelessness means that you are knowledgeable of firearm safety rules, but fail to apply them one hundred percent of the time.

Safe gun handling is your responsibility, and safety must always be your concern. To ensure the safe use of any firearm, always follow these four general safety rules:

Rule #1: Always assume a firearm is loaded
Whenever you touch any firearm, you must always assume it's loaded and must immediately open the action of the weapon and look into the chamber to see if it is clear of ammunition. Keep in mind that semiautomatic guns will require you to first remove the magazine before opening the action.

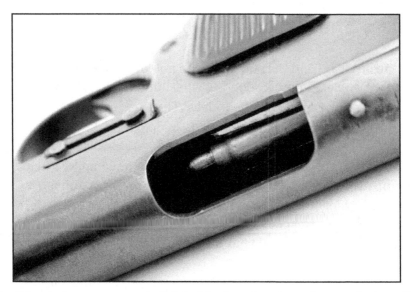

In this photo, we see a bullet inside the chamber of a semiautomatic handgun.

With a revolver, you must open the cylinder completely to be certain it is clear of ammunition.

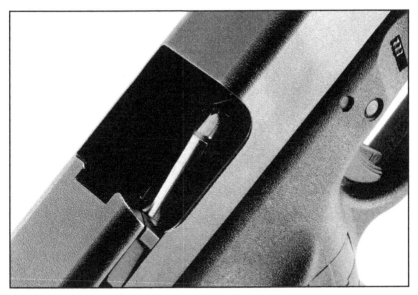

With semiautomatic guns, people often remove the magazine but forget there is still a round left in the chamber of the gun. Remember, you must always pull the slide back and look into the chamber for any ammunition.

Rule #2: Always point a firearm in a safe direction

This is by far the most important gun safety rule because if the firearm is unintentionally discharged, it will not cause injury or death. Essentially, a "safe direction" means the gun is pointed in a direction that will not cause injury to anyone. Adhering to this critical safety rule will require you to be cognizant of where your muzzle (front end) is pointing at all times.

In this photo, a member of the Israeli military takes a break from his watch. Notice what direction the muzzle of his weapon is pointing.

Rule #3: Always know what is beyond your target

Regardless of the situation, you must always be absolutely sure of your target and know exactly what is beyond it before you squeeze the trigger. This means you must be certain that your chosen target has an effective backstop that will prevent the bullet from causing collateral damage. This can be particularly problematic when shooting in real world environments (i.e., home invasion situation, street altercation, etc).

Before you shoot, you must be absolutely certain that your chosen target has an effective backstop that will prevent the bullet from causing collateral damage.

"Most firearm accidents are attributed to ignorance and carelessness."

Unlike real world environments, the gun range will provide you with an effective backstop that will safely stop the bullet.

Rule #4: Never put your finger on the trigger until you are ready to shoot.

Despite what some anti gun activists might want you to believe, guns do not just "go off" by themselves. It requires a human to squeeze the trigger or somehow activate the action of the gun to strike the primer of the bullet.

Because of the unique ergonomics of a gun combined with the human instinct to lead our hand grasp with our index finger, there's a natural tendency for people to want to place their index finger on the trigger of a gun. You must avoid this and train yourself to always keep your finger outside the trigger guard until you are ready to shoot. The best place to keep your index finger is straight along the frame of the gun

Keeping your finger off the trigger is a universal safety rule followed by both military and law enforcement personnel.

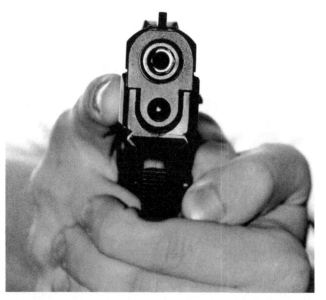

Until you are ready to shoot, you must keep your index finger firmly placed against the side of the frame of the weapon.

32

"While all of the firearm safety rules are important, never forget the most important rule: Always point a firearm in a safe direction. So if the firearm is unintentionally discharged, it will not cause injury or death."

While the four standard gun safety rules must be put into practice one hundred percent of the time, here are several firearm safety rules you should also put into action:

- Always read the owner's manual that comes with your firearm.

- Always be sure the barrel of your gun is clear of obstructions.

- Always use clean, dry factory-made ammunition of the proper caliber.

- Always wear ear protection and safety glasses when practicing at the firing range.

- Do not leave an unattended gun loaded.

- Never allow your firearm to be used by anyone who is not knowledgeable of the safety rules.

- Never trust a safety.

- Before cleaning your firearm, make sure that the chamber is empty, and be absolutely certain it is unloaded.

- Always make sure that all ammunition is stored away from the cleaning area.

- Never use alcohol or drugs before or while shooting.

- Always store guns so they are not accessible to untrained or unauthorized persons.

- Always be certain your firearm is safe to operate.

- Never fire at surfaces that can cause your bullet to ricochet.

- Always comply with the safety regulations of your firing range.

"Safe gun handling is your responsibility, and safety must always be your concern."

Alcohol and guns and a very dangerous mix. Never handle a firearm if you are drinking!

Is this person practicing safe gun handling?

"If you are considering owning a gun you must never forget that firearm ownership is a full-time responsibility."

35

Children and Firearms

It is the responsibility of every parent to be a positive role model for their children. Always practice safe gun handling. It is also important to talk openly about guns with your children.

Do not make firearms a taboo subject. Doing so can elicit children's curiosity and possibly lead them to investigate guns on their own. Even if you're not a gun owner, your son or daughter may one day come in contact with a firearm at a relative or friend's house.

The best time to talk about gun safety is when your child begins to show interest, e.g., when your son begins to act out gun scenes or your daughter becomes curious and asks questions.

As a rule of thumb, you can discuss firearms safety with children as young as 7 years of age. However, the amount of information and training that you give your child will depend upon three important factors:

- The child's age.

- The child's level of maturity.

- The child's ability to reason.

Do not make firearms a taboo subject. Doing so can elicit children's curiosity and possibly lead them to investigate guns on their own.

When discussing firearms with your children, be certain to answer all of their questions. If you don't know an answer to a particular question, speak with a qualified firearms instructor or a knowledgeable law enforcement officer.

One of the most important principles to teach your children is to be safe around guns. Instruct them to never handle a gun unless you are with them and only when you give them permission.

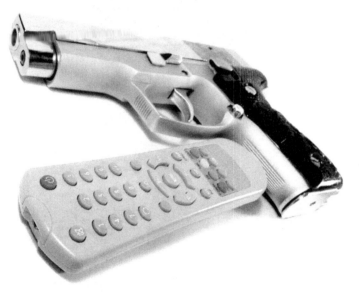

There is no escaping gun violence in movies and television.

Luckily, the National Rifle Association (NRA) has created a gun accident prevention program called Eddie Eagle for children from preschool through third grade who are generally considered too young to be allowed to handle firearms. If ever your child finds a gun in your absence, the Eddie Eagle program teaches them the following four safety rules:

1. Stop where you are.

2. Don't touch the gun.

3. Leave immediately.

4. Tell a trustworthy adult.

It is very important to recite these with your children until they memorize them.

If your child is old enough to own a BB gun you must teach him or her the standard firearm safety rules.

AGE	ACTIONS TO BE TAKEN
2-6 years	Children should be exposed to the Eddie Eagle Program and learn what to do when exposed to a firearm in your absence.
7-12 years	Depending on your child's level of maturity, teach him the standard firearm safety rules. If they own a BB gun make certain they consistently employ the gun safety rules.
Teenagers	Teenagers who have mastered the standard safety rules and who demonstrate the necessary maturity can learn how to operate a real firearm.

Fantasy and Reality

Since guns and shoot-out scenes are common in TV, movies and video games, it is also important for you to explain the differences between fact and fantasy. Tell your children that actors use play guns and pretend to die. Then explain that your firearm is real, very dangerous, and should never be treated as a toy. Again, answer any questions that they ask.

Some video games can be extremely violent and can exposes your children to a tremendous amount of gun violence.

CHAPTER THREE

Gun Basics

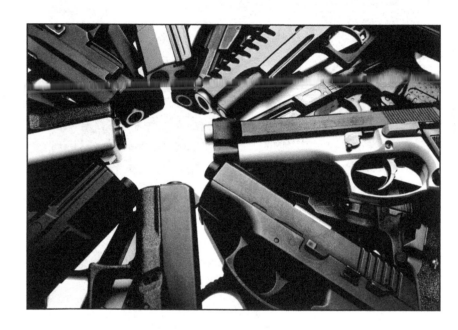

The 3 Basic Types of Guns

For self defense purposes, there are three basic types of guns to consider: shotguns, revolvers, and semiautomatics. Let's first take a look at shotguns.

Shotguns

Just about everyone can agree that shotguns have tremendous stopping power. Absent a miracle or some extraordinary anomaly, a shotgun blast at close range usually guarantees instant death.

Accuracy Counts with a Shotgun

Many people mistakingly assume that a shotgun is the preferred weapon for home defense because you don't need to be accurate when shooting. *This assumption is wrong.* For example, shooting a target at close proximity (approximately 7 to 10 feet) with a shotgun will only create a hole the size of a baseball. It's very possible you can miss your target under the stressful conditions of a self defense situation. You therefore need to be accurate if you intend on hitting your target with a shotgun. Yes, accuracy counts with a shotgun!

Shotguns shoot slugs and shot. Slugs are round lead balls that vary in size. Shot is a package or wad of metal balls that vary in size and spread out as they travel away from the muzzle. For self defense purposes, the ideal shot size should be either oo or ooo. Some old school shooters claim that shot has a benefit of reducing the need for pin point accuracy, but the truth is you must be accurate with any firearm. Keep in mind that a shot-loaded shotgun is not the weapon you need if you're looking at a hostage situation. You're going to need something with a capability for surgical precision. In addition, shotguns are easy to load, unload and fire. Compared to handguns, they are, on the whole, cheaper and easier to buy. They are also less regulated than handguns. Overall, I recommend a 12-gauge. It's what the police use.

A shotgun slug is often used for hunting large game.

One disadvantage of a shotgun is its "kick" or recoil. A 12-gauge shotgun with a hot combat load can knock you down if you're not properly braced when you trip it off. Another disadvantage of a shotgun is its size and length. You really can't carry it around with you. A shotgun can also be difficult to maneuver in close quarter environments. Because it's a long barreled weapon, a criminal assailant can more easily grab the barrel for disarming purposes. Remember, the idea that guns increase your range of attack. Try not to forfeit the strategic advantage through use of a shotgun.

Pictured here, a BB Shot that contains 50 BB pellets per ounce of shot.

00 Shot contains 8 pellets per ounce of shot and is an ideal load for home defense.

There are a wide variety of tactical shotguns available on the market. It's best to spend time researching the pros and cons of each model before making a purchase.

Handguns

Some experts argue that handguns are the superior weapon for personal protection. Unlike long guns (shotguns and rifles), handguns (with practice and training) can be transported, drawn, and fired very quickly. Handguns can, if necessary, even be shot with one hand. There are two types of handguns: revolvers and semiautomatics. Let's first take a look at the revolver.

Unlike the semiautomatic pistol, it's much easier to tell if a revolver is loaded with ammunition. Simply, depress the cylinder release latch, pop open the cylinder and make a visual inspection of each chamber

The Revolver

Some people consider the revolver the best type of firearm for personal protection. It is called a revolver because its cylinder revolves when the trigger is pulled. Revolvers hold anywhere from five to nine cartridges, depending upon the cylinder. They also come in single action (you have to cock the hammer before it can be fired) or double action (you just squeeze the trigger). Loading a revolver is safe and simple, and you can easily tell when it has rounds in it. They almost never jam, and they can be trusted to fire effectively.

The operation of a revolver is incredibly simple. Simply squeeze the trigger (assuming it's a double action revolver) or cock the hammer back and it will rotate the cylinder and align a round of ammunition between the hammer and the barrel of the gun.

The number of rounds a revolver can hold will vary. In this photo, this .38 special holds 5 rounds of ammunition in its cylinder.

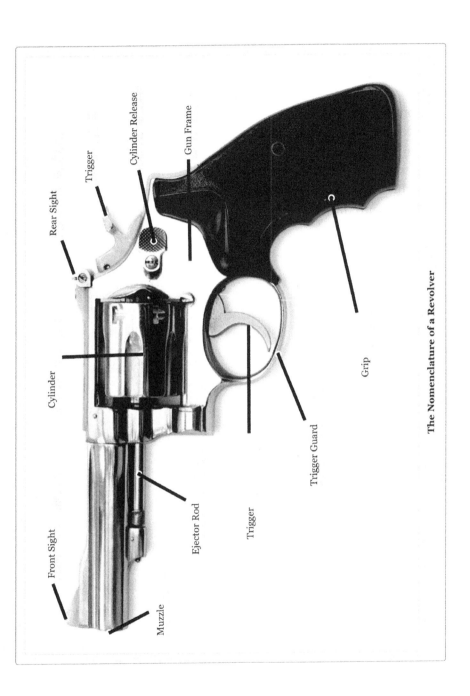

Rear Sight

Trigger

Cylinder Release

Gun Frame

Cylinder

Front Sight

Muzzle

Ejector Rod

Trigger

Trigger Guard

Grip

The Nomenclature of a Revolver

The Semiautomatic

The Semiautomatic pistols differ from revolvers in many ways. They are called "semiautomatics" because when fired they automatically feed a fresh round and eject the spent casing. All you have to do is keep squeezing the trigger. Most full automatics require you to squeeze the trigger once, thus emptying the entire magazine. With the semiautomatic, rounds are loaded vertically in a metal container called the magazine. The magazine is then inserted into the grip of the gun.

One of the main advantages to a semiautomatic pistol is that you can load and reload it very quickly by ejecting the empty magazine and sliding a full magazine back into its place. This type of handgun carries a lot more rounds than a revolver. This is an important consideration when you're confronted by multiple armed attackers. Semiautomatics generally have a lighter trigger pull weight than their revolver cousins, and this can make a difference in accuracy under pressure.

In short, semiautomatics hold more ammunition, can be fired faster, and can be reloaded faster. They are really the ideal weapon for combat, as you might imagine. On the other hand, they are generally more complicated than revolvers. And some experts say they are more dangerous than revolvers because it's harder to know readily if they're loaded.

With the semiautomatic, rounds are loaded vertically in a metal container called the magazine. The magazine is then inserted into the grip of the gun.

For personal protection, I prefer the 9mm SIG Sauer P226 combat pistol. It is known for its excellent accuracy, feeding reliability and incapacitation potential. The SIG Sauer P226 has a barrel length of 4.41 inches, weighs approximately 26.5 ounces, and has a magazine capacity of 15 rounds. It has a 12-pound trigger pull on double action and a 4-pound trigger pull on single action.

One of the best features of the SIG Sauer P226 is its moderate recoil. It's no wonder that the SIG Sauer is quickly becoming a favorite weapon among many law enforcement agencies.

Please remember that no matter what kind of gun you buy - if you get one - it isn't going to help you unless you know what you're doing. Get trained by a qualified instructor in firearm personal protection and never forget the fundamental rules of firearm safety.

Pictured here, a SIG Sauer semiautomatic handgun with the slide in the rear locked position. With the action of the weapon open, you are now able to inspect the chamber for ammunition.

How to Check if a Semiautomatic Is Loaded

- Always start off with your finger off the trigger and the gun pointed in a safe direction.

- Next, eject the magazine from the grip of the gun.

- While holding the gun firmly with one hand, use your other hand to grasp the slide of the gun and pull it back to the rear locking position.

- Once the slide is in the locked position, visually inspect the chamber and make certain there is no ammunition present. You may also insert your little finger into the chamber to make certain it is empty.

- Remember, a semiautomatic handgun is only considered to be unloaded when the magazine has been removed and the chamber of the gun is empty.

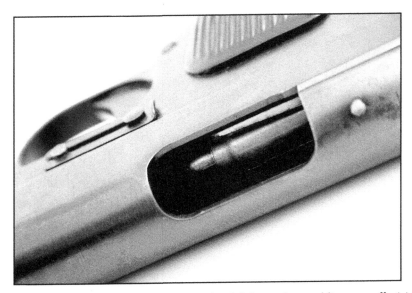

Unlike the revolver, the semiautomatic pistol requires a bit more effort to see if the weapon is loaded. To check if a semiautomatic is loaded, a proper sequence of steps must always be followed.

Semiautomatic magazines come in a wide variety of sizes.

Pictured here, the hammer on a semiautomatic pistol.

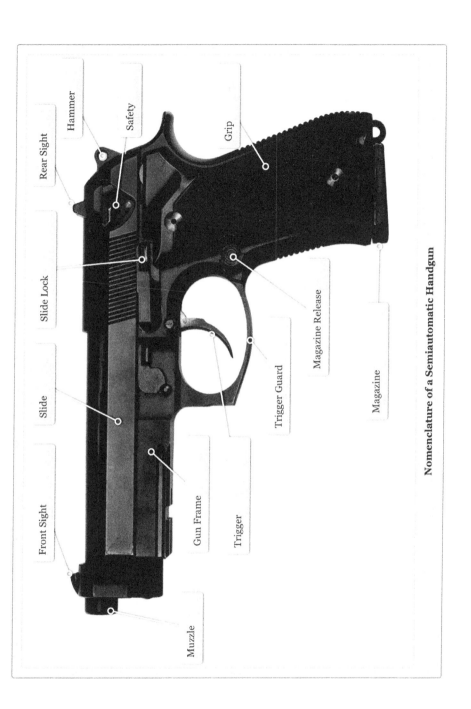

Nomenclature of a Semiautomatic Handgun

Hammer

Safety

Rear Sight

Grip

Slide Lock

Slide

Front Sight

Magazine Release

Magazine

Trigger Guard

Gun Frame

Trigger

Muzzle

55

Handgun Ammunition

Firearm ammunition is often referred to as either a *round* or *cartridge*. Essentially, a cartridge consists of four basic parts. Let's take a look at each one and its function.

Metal casing - this is a metallic case that provides the structure of the cartridge and it's made precisely to fit the firing chamber of a firearm. Essentially, the case holds the bullet, powder and primer.

Primer - is a small charge of an impact-sensitive chemical compound located at the bottom of the case. When struck by the firing pin it ignites the powder charge.

Powder charge - burns rapidly and produces a large volume of gas in the case.

Projectile - the expanding gas in the case drives the bullet out of the case and through the barrel at an extremely high rate of speed.

There are also two different types of cartridges that can be used for both handgun and rifles:

Rimfire - the chemical primer is located on the bottom rim of the case.

Centerfire - the chemical primer is located in the center of the case bottom.

Pictured here, a 9mm centerfire cartridge. Notice the indentation in the center of the case that is created from the firing pin.

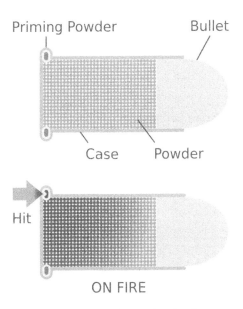

A schematic of a rimfire cartridge. Illustration by Arz.

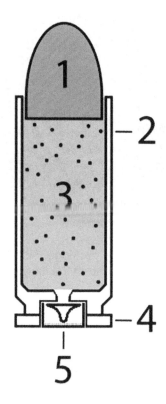

A schematic of a centerfire cartridge.

1. Projectile
2. Metal Casing
3. Powder charge
4. Rim
5. Primer

Anatomy of a Cartridge

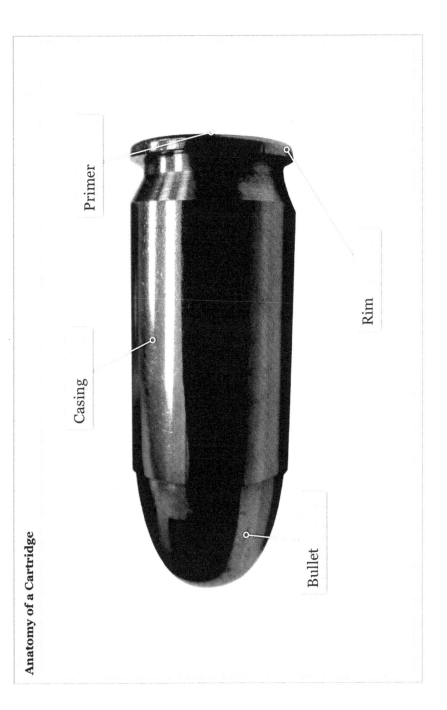

Primer

Casing

Rim

Bullet

Firing Sequence

It's important you to understand exactly how ammunition fires or what is also known as ammunition firing sequence. When you squeeze the trigger or a pistol, rifle or shotgun the following sequence of events will occur:

- The firing pin of the firearm will strike the impact sensitive primer, causing it to ignite.

- The priming compound creates a flame that ignites the power charge.

- The powder charge ignites fast and generates a high volume of gas.

- The rapidly expanding gas then pushes the bullet out of the cartridge casing.

- The bullet is then propelled out of the barrel of the firearm at an extremely high rate of speed.

Full Metal Jacket and Hollow-Point Ammunition

The type of ammunition that you select is just as important as the firearm that you choose for self defense. This brings us to the choice between full metal jacket and hollow-point ammunition.

Full Metal Jacket Bullets

Full metal jacket or FMJ is a bullet consisting of a soft lead core encased by a copper sheath. Because of its design, FMJ bullets will generally not expand upon impact with its target. As a result, this bullet will often pierce right through its target resulting in minimal target damage.

60

More importantly, in a self defense situation, a full metal jacket bullet can easily penetrate a criminal's body and then hit and innocent bystander. It's no wonder that in 1998, all major police departments in the United States switched from FMJ to Hollow-Point ammunition.

Full Metal Jacket Ammunition

Hollow-Point Bullets

Hollow-points are expanding bullets that are hollowed out at their tip. They are designed this way to help prevent over-penetration with their intended target. For self defense purposes, the hollow point round is ideal because it minimizes the chances of your bullet exiting from the intended target and harming an innocent bystander.

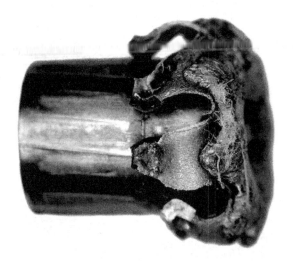

Pictured here, a side view of a .38 Special hollow-point bullet. Notice the "mushrooming" that occurs when the bullet reaches its target.

Essentially, a hollow-point round will expand or "mushroom" when it hits its target. This is especially important for three of the following reasons:

1. The bullet will have decreased penetration which helps minimize collateral damage. Preventing over-penetration is especially important for people who live or work in restricted or heavily crowded environments such as police officers.

2. The bullet has better stopping power because it damages more tissue which leads to greater blood loss and shock. Hollow-point ammunition is much safer than full metal jacket rounds and are therefore standard issue in just about every police department.

3. Unlike full metal jacket ammo, hollow-point bullets transfer all of its kinetic energy into its target.

Pictured here, an expanded .40 S&W bullet next to a hollow-point round. Photo by Oleg Volk.

To prevent over penetration with its intended target, all police agencies are required to use hollow-point ammunition.

Ammunition Care and Storage

Believe it or not, ammunition care and storage is just as important as caring for your firearm. What follows is a list of important points to remember:

- Never forget that firearm ammunition contains explosive ingredients that are dangerous. It should always be treated with care in handling and storage.

- Only use ammunition recommended for your firearm by its manufacturer.

- If you do not use your firearm for home defense, you should store your ammunition separately from your gun.

- Always store your ammunition in a cool and dry location, approximate temperature range of 50 to 80 degrees. Avoid extreme temperature ranges.

- Keep water, gun solvents, oils, paint thinner, petroleum products and all liquids away from ammunition.

- Get into the habit of routinely inspecting your ammunition before using it. Immediately discard any ammunition that shows signs of corrosion.

- To avoid projectile setback, avoid the tendency to chamber and un-chamber the same round multiple times.

- Ammunition should be stored in its original factory box or packaging. The factory labeling and identification on the original box will help match it with the correct firearm.

Malfunctions

No weapon is one hundred percent fool-proof! While just about all firearms are extremely reliable, there is the possibility that your weapon will fail to fire properly. In most cases, this can be attributed to a problem with the ammunition.

For all practical purposes, there are three types of ammunition malfunctions: They are:

- **Misfire** - the cartridge fails to fire after the primer has been struck by the firing pin.

- **Hangfire** - there is a noticeable and unexpected delay in the ignition of a cartridge after the primer has been stuck.

- **Squib Load** - there is less than normal pressure after the cartridge has ignited. As a result, the bullet exits the casing but there isn't enough force to send it out of the barrel of the gun.

Dealing with a Misfire and Hangfire

If you come across a situation when the round fails to fire immediately after you have squeezed the trigger you might have either a misfire or hangfire malfunction. *It's critical that you keep the gun pointed in a safe direction as the gun can still fire if it's a hangfire.* Also, wait at least 30 seconds before attempting to open the action to remove the defective cartridge.

Pictured here, the residual of a hangfire malfunction. Photo by Mika Järvinen

Dealing with a Squib Load

If you noticed a reduced recoil or unusual sound when firing your gun, a squib load might have been fired. Again, keep your gun pointed in a safe direction and wait 30 seconds before opening the action to unload the gun. Also, check carefully that the chamber and barrel of the gun are empty. You should carefully run a cleaning rod through the barrel of the gun to be certain there is nothing obstructing it.

Warning! An unidentified squib load can be extremely dangerous for the shooter! If a bullet is lodged in the barrel of your gun and you fire another shot, it can result in a serious injury and certainly damage your firearm.

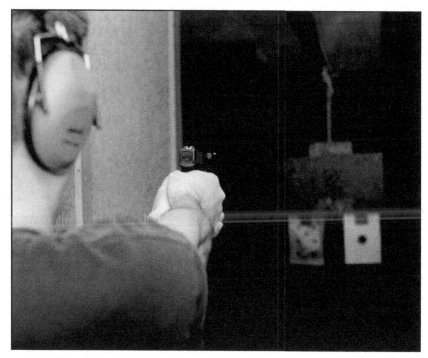

If you encounter a situation when the round fails to fire immediately after you have squeezed the trigger, you might have either a misfire or hangfire malfunction. It's critical that you keep the gun pointed in a safe direction as the gun can still fire if it's a hangfire.

Choosing the Right Gun

One of the most common questions my students ask is, "what is the best handgun for self defense?" Well, in order to answer this question I have to explain the importance of handgun caliber. Essentially, the term "Caliber" refers to the size designations for bullets and the inside diameters of the gun barrels. Also keep in mind that "Caliber" is expressed in units of either inches or millimeters (mm).

For example, a designation like .22, .308, .32, .357, .44, .45, etc refers the approximate outside diameter, in inches, of the bullet and the inside diameter of the barrel. Its also worth mentioning that "Gauge" is a term for size designations of shot shells (for shotguns).

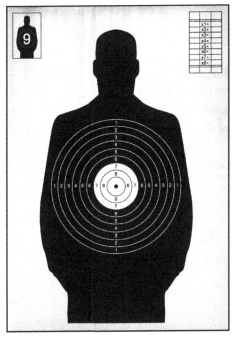

Regardless of which caliber gun you choose, you will need consistent training to sharpen your skills.

Here are a few self defense handgun calibers for review:

.38 Caliber Pistol

The .38 caliber measure thirty-eight hundredths of an inch in diameter. This was a standard round for most law enforcement agencies from 1930's through the 1960's. In fact, the .38 caliber revolvers have been in service since World War II.

Because of its limited round capacity and poor stopping power, the .38 round is not recommended for self defense and personal protection.

9mm Pistol

The 9mm is a popular cartridge was designed to operate in semi automatic and full auto firearms, and is used worldwide by elite military units. The 9mm is the current NATO standard caliber for handgun cartridges.

The 9mm is a great round because of its large shot capacity, low recoil and sufficient stopping power. This cartridge is still one of my personal favorites for self defense. For some of you skeptics who think the 9mm does not have sufficient stopping power - think again. Its merely an issue of using the right cartridge. For example, did you know there is 9mm ammunition that will give you the stopping power of a .45 handgun.

.40 Caliber Pistol

The .40 S&W round was essentially designed as a law enforcement cartridge. For some people, the .40 is a middle ground caliber. The .40 round seems to have a bit more muzzle energy than a 9mm and less flash and recoil of a .357 round. This is certainly a good caliber for self defense purposes.

.357 Magnum Pistol

The .357 Magnum cartridge was developed by Elmer Keith and Smith & Wesson in 1934. While the .357 Magnum was primarily created for hunting, it was quickly adopted by law enforcement, who needed a round with increased effectiveness against criminals in automobiles. Because of its impressive stopping power, the .357 Magnum is an excellent self defense round. However, keep in mind that this gun will have significant recoil kick back.

.45 Caliber Pistol

This is a "work horse" round that has been around since World War I. The .45 round is well known for its accuracy and stopping power and is considered to be one of the world's more effective self defense handgun cartridges. It has been said that getting shot by a .45 is likened to someone throwing a manhole cover into your chest! It's no wonder the .45 ACP pistol round is often referred to as a "manstopper."

What about the .22 Caliber Pistol for Self Defense?

.22 Caliber Pistol

When it comes to handguns for self defense, the .22 caliber pistol is not a desirable weapon. While this popular caliber might be great for target practice, it simply doesn't have the stopping power necessary to stop a crazed criminal attacker in his tracks. While it's true that people have died from a .22 caliber gunshot, the round will not reliably stop the immediate threat and in most cases you can get hurt or killed during the altercation.

Reliable stopping power is one of the most important prerequisites of handgun self defense. Essentially, "stopping power" describes a firearms ability to penetrate and immediately incapacitate or "stop" a human target.

"One of the most important prerequisites for handgun self defense is reliable stopping power."

Stopping power describes a firearms ability to penetrate and immediately incapacitate or stop a human target from continuing deadly aggression.

CHAPTER FOUR

Gun Maintenance

Cleaning Your Gun

One important aspect of gun maintenance is knowing how to properly clean your weapon. Regular firearm cleaning is important for some of the following important reasons:

This will ensure that your firearm will fire properly. However, if you discover there is a problem with the weapon, take it to a gunsmith or contact the manufacturer directly. *Do not attempt to repair it yourself.*

Regular cleaning will help protect the gun's value. Firearms are not cheap and will only hold their value if you take care of them, keep them clean and keep them in proper working order.

It helps familiarize you with the weapon's nomenclature. Regular cleaning will make you more familiar with the various parts of your firearm.

When cleaning your firearm, you must remember to always apply the safety rules. Most importantly, *you must make certain the firearm is unloaded and remember to remove all ammunition from where you are cleaning the weapon. Also, avoid consuming alcohol when clearing your gun.*

Alcohol and guns do not mix! Remember, never consume alcohol when cleaning your weapon.

Gun Cleaning Supplies

You will need the following items to effectively clean your firearm. They include some of the following:

- Cleaning rod

- Bore brush

- Cloth cleaning patches

- Bore cleaning solvent

- Gun oil

- Small cleaning brush

You can buy gun cleaning supplies from your local gun dealer as well as the internet. However, make certain that the bore brush is the correct caliber or gauge size for your firearm.

Gun Cleaning Procedure

Cleaning your gun is a relatively easy process that can be accomplished in a short period of time. Once again, before you begin, make certain the gun is *unloaded* and all *ammunition has been removed from the area.*

- Depending on the firearm, disassemble your gun so you have full access to all of its parts. However, keep in mind that some guns (revolvers) cannot be disassembled at all.

- Attach the bore brush to the cleaning rod.

- Dip the bore bush in the bore cleaning solvent.

- Place several drops of cleaning solvent in the bore of the gun.

- Insert the brush through the end of the barrel and work the bore brush back and forth in a smooth and controlled motion to loosen the residue. Make certain to push the brush through the entire length of the bore, approximately 4 times.

- Disconnect the bore brush and attach the cloth cleaning patch to the rod. Run several of the cloth patches through the bore until they come out dry and clean.

- Once the bore is dry and clean, run a lightly oiled patch through the bore.

- Next, take a small cleaning bush and clean the dirt and residue from the gun's action.

- Finally, wipe the entire surface of the gun with a light coat of oil.

Cleaning your gun will provide you with a greater understanding of the weapon's nomenclature. Pictured here, a field-stripped semiautomatic pistol ready to be cleaned.

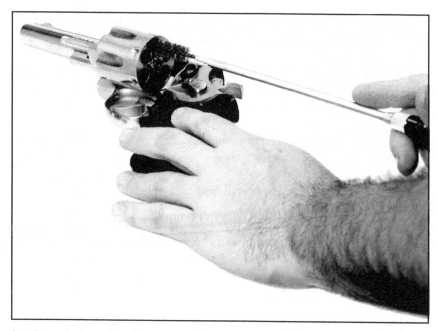

In this photo, cleaning a revolver with a bore brush attached to a cleaning rod. Notice how the user keeps his fingers off the trigger when cleaning his weapon.

Safe Gun Storage

The next aspect of proper gun maintenance is safe storage. As a responsible gun owner, you must make certain your weapon is stored in a safe manner. Failure to do so can possibly lead to a tragic accident in your home.

Three Objectives of Safe Gun Storage

Safe gun storage should accomplish the following three objectives:

1. *They must not be accessible to untrained or unauthorized persons.*

2. *Prevent the gun from firing.*

3. *Protect the gun from damage.*

There are two components that make up safe storage of a firearm. They are:

• Storage Location

• Storage Device

Storage Location
There are several factors that must be considered when choosing the ideal location, such as ease of access, personal needs, self defense readiness and environmental conditions.

Regardless of where you store your guns, there is one critical rule that must always be followed: *All firearms must be stored so they are not accessible to untrained or unauthorized persons.*

There are several factors you must take into consideration when choosing where and how to store your gun. One important factor is how many untrained and unauthorized people live in your home?

Here are some important question you will need to ask yourself before choosing a storage location for your guns:

1. What is the firearm used for (i.e., hunting, collecting, self defense, etc)?

2. How many firearms do you own?

3. What type of firearms do you own (i.e., handgun, rifle, shotgun, etc)?

4. How many untrained and unauthorized people live in your home?

5. Do you have children and have they been taught firearm safety?

6. Will your firearm be used for home defense purposes?

7. Do you live in a high-crime area?

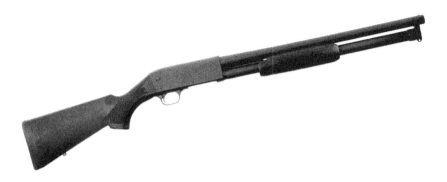

The type of firearm you own is also an important factor when determining how and where you will store it.

Storage Devices

There are a wide variety of gun storage devices available, however keep in mind that not all of these storage options will prevent unauthorized access to your weapon. Some of the popular storage devices include:

- Trigger Locks

- Cable Locks

- Plastic or Fabric Cases

- Strong Boxes

- Steel Gun Cabinets

- Gun Safes

Trigger Locks

Trigger locks are simply designed to keep your gun from discharging by preventing the trigger from being pressed. They offer the bare minimum in safe gun storage.

A close-up photo of a trigger lock.

While a trigger lock will stop someone from discharging the gun, it will not prevent a thief from stealing it and bypassing the lock later.

Cable Locks

Cable locks require you to thread a heavy duty cable through the barrel or action of the firearm. Essentially, this prevents the action from cycling completely. Once again, all gun locks are considered the least effective device for safe gun storage.

Pictured here, a cable lock used on a Glock semiautomatic handgun.

Plastic or Fabric Gun Cases

Because of its weak structural integrity, both plastic and fabric gun cases do not qualify as a safe storage option. However, these gun cases are ideal for transporting your gun to the range or gunsmith. Again, *plastic and cloth gun cases do not offer secure gun storage and will not prevent untrained or unauthorized persons from gaining access.*

Pictured here, a typical plastic gun case.

Pictured here, a soft gun case.

Strong Boxes

Strong boxes offer decent security for your handgun while also offering the portability of a plastic or fabric case. Most strong boxes offer reliable locking mechanisms and can be permanently mounted to floors or walls.

Best of all, many strong boxes offer electronic push-button access and biometric locks that can provide immediate access. This is particularly important to those who will rely on their firearm for home security and personal protection.

Pictured here, a push-button strong box.

Gun Safes

Gun Safes are, without a doubt, the most secure gun storage options available. Unlike the strong box, the gun safes will allow you to secure your long guns (i.e., rifles and shotguns) as well as your handguns.

Many gun safes have plush interiors and built-in racks that will help to preserve the finish of your weapons. Most importantly, gun safes are effective theft deterrents.

There are a few disadvantages of gun safes. They are very large, extremely heavy, difficult to install and expensive. Nevertheless, they are the ideal security solution for many gun owners.

Gun safes are the most secure gun storage option available to the consumer.

Firearm Storage and Home Security

As a general firearm safety rule, ammunition should always be separated from the storage location of your gun. However, this safety rule presents a unique problem for many gun owners who rely on their weapon for home defense and personal protection.

For example, in a home invasion situation you must have immediate access to your weapon and it must always be loaded and ready to fire at a seconds notice. When it comes to self defense, an unloaded gun is a useless gun!

If you are going to rely on a gun for home defense you might want to keep it loaded and stored in a locked strong box, hidden in a special location that you can gain quick access.

The truth is you must weigh and consider all the factors that relate to your individual needs and circumstances and choose a practical and responsible way to secure your gun.

About the Author

Sammy Franco is one of the world's foremost authorities on armed and unarmed combat. Highly regarded as a leading innovator in combat sciences, Mr. Franco was one of the premier pioneers in the field of "reality-based" self-defense.

Convinced of the limited usefulness of martial arts in real street fighting situations, Mr. Franco believes in the theory that the best way to change traditional thinking is to make antiquated ideas obsolete through superior methodology. His innovative ideas have made a significant contribution to changing the thinking of many in the field about how people can best defend themselves against vicious and formidable adversaries.

Sammy Franco is perhaps best known as the founder and creator of Contemporary Fighting Arts (CFA), a state-of-the-art offensive-based combat system that is specifically designed for real-world self-defense. CFA is a sophisticated and practical system of self-defense, designed specifically to provide efficient and effective methods to avoid, defuse, confront, and neutralize both armed and unarmed attackers.

After studying and training in numerous martial art systems and related disciplines and acquiring extensive firsthand experience from real "street" combat, Mr. Franco developed his first system, known as Analytical Street Fighting. This system, which was one of the first practical "street fighting" martial arts, employed an unrestrained reality-based training methodology known as Simulated Street Fighting. Analytical Street Fighting served as the foundation for the fundamental principles of Contemporary Fighting Arts and Mr. Franco's teaching methodology.

CFA also draws from the concepts and principles of numerous sciences and disciplines, including police and military science, criminal justice, criminology, sociology, human psychology, philosophy, histrionics, kinesics, proxemics, kinesiology, emergency medicine, crisis management, and human anatomy.

Sammy Franco has frequently been featured in martial art magazines, newspapers, and appeared on numerous radio and television programs. Mr. Franco has also authored numerous books, magazine articles and editorials, and has developed a popular library of instructional DVDs and workout music. As a matter of fact, his book Street Lethal was one of the first books ever published on the subject of reality based self defense. His other books include Killer Instinct, When Seconds Count, 1001 Street Fighting Secrets, First Strike, The Bigger They Are – The Harder They Fall, War Machine, War Craft, Ground War, Warrior Wisdom, Heavy Bag Training, and Out of the Cage.

Sammy Franco's experience and credibility in the combat science is unequaled. One of his many accomplishments in this field includes the fact that he has earned the ranking of a Law Enforcement Master Instructor, and has designed, implemented, and taught officer survival training to the United States Border Patrol (USBP). He instructs members of the US Secret Service, Military Special Forces, Washington DC Police Department, Montgomery County, Maryland Deputy Sheriffs, and the US Library of Congress Police. Sammy Franco is also a member of the prestigious International Law Enforcement Educators and Trainers Association (ILEETA) as well as the American Society of Law Enforcement Trainers (ASLET) and he is listed in the "Who's Who Director of Law Enforcement Instructors."

Sammy Franco is a nationally certified Law Enforcement Instructor in the following curricula: PR-24 Side-Handle Baton, Police Arrest and Control Procedures, Police Personal Weapons Tactics, Police Power Handcuffing Methods, Police Oleoresin Capsicum Aerosol Training (OCAT), Police Weapon Retention and

Disarming Methods, Police Edged Weapon Countermeasures and "Use of Force" Assessment and Response Methods.

Mr. Franco is also a National Rifle Association (NRA) instructor who specializes in firearm safety, personal protection and advanced combat pistol shooting.

Mr. Franco holds a Bachelor of Arts degree in Criminal Justice from the University of Maryland. He is a regularly featured speaker at a number of professional conferences, and conducts dynamic and enlightening seminars on numerous aspects of self defense and personal protection.

Mr. Franco has instructed thousands of students in his career, including instruction on street fighting, grappling and ground fighting, boxing and kickboxing, knife combat, multiple opponent survival skills, stick fighting, and firearms training. Having lived through street violence himself, Mr. Franco's goal is not its glorification, but to help people free themselves from violence and its costly price.

For more information about Mr. Franco and his Contemporary Fighting Arts system, you can visit his websites at:

www.sammyfranco.com and

www.contemporaryfightingarts.com

NOTES

Made in the USA
Coppell, TX
26 July 2022

80464095R00056